Fun in the Sun

By Debbie Croft

I am hot! I can dip.

It is fun to dip in the sun.

Jac did a fun run.

Jac got a bib.

She had fun on the run!

Sam and Jip go for a run.

Jip can tug!

Dad and Peg get a bat.

Peg hits and hits.

Peg and Dad had fun.

Mum is fit.

She can jog.

But she gets hot.

Pip can go up and up.

She did not hit the net!

Tim did hip hop in the sun.

Tim had fun.

Mog naps on the mat.

Mog has fun in the sun!

CHECKING FOR MEANING

1. What are two different ways to have fun in the sun? *(Literal)*

2. How did Jac have fun in the sun? *(Literal)*

3. Why does Jip tug when he goes for a run? *(Inferential)*

EXTENDING VOCABULARY

dip	What does it mean to *dip*? If you have a dip in the water, do you spend a short or a long time in the water? What are other meanings of the word *dip*?
tug	What does it mean to *tug*? What does Jip do when he tugs on the lead? What does a tugboat do to help big ships?
jog	When Mum jogs, what does she do? Does she move quickly or slowly? What is another word that has a similar meaning to *jog*?

MOVING BEYOND THE TEXT

1. What are some other activities people do in the sun to have fun?

2. How should you protect your skin when you are outside playing in the sun?

3. Why is it healthy to do activities outside?

4. What outdoor activity would you like to do that you have never tried? Why would it be fun?

SPEED SOUNDS

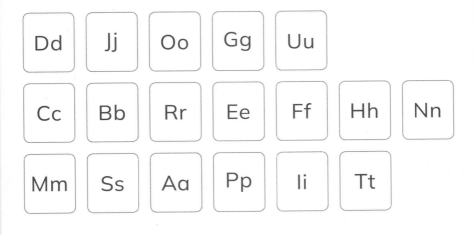

Dd	Jj	Oo	Gg	Uu

Cc	Bb	Rr	Ee	Ff	Hh	Nn

Mm	Ss	Aa	Pp	Ii	Tt

sun

hot

dip

fun

got

had

did

run

Peg

Jip

tug

but

Mum

Dad

get

gets

and

jog

did

Mog

Jac

But

not

hop

up

on